haiku yellow

Haiku Yellow

This collection is published by Lost Tower Publications.

LTP publish a wide range of poetry and fiction titles and are renowned for passion, quality and individuality.

©2016 by Lost Tower Publications

For further information, please visit:
http://losttowerpublications.jigsy.com

Poetry Collections by P.J. Reed

The Wicked Come

Haiku Nation

Frozen Haiku

Haiku Yellow

haiku yellow

Biography

P.J. Reed is a writer and poet from England. She holds a BAEd from Canterbury Christ Church University and an MA from Bradford University. She is an eclectic writer; her work ranging from romantic poetry to Gothic horror novels. Her work has found its way into a wide variety of international anthologies, journals, Zines and writing guides.

She has published one collection of dark romantic and Gothic horror poetry entitled *The Wicked Come*.

Her high fantasy novel *The Torcian Chronicles* will be published in 2017. As a counterbalance to her dark writing, P.J. also writes of the beauty and ethereal nature of the changing countryside in her series of haiku inspired collections.

Her first haiku collection, *Haiku Nation*, is a magical collection of powerful, modern haiku.

Her winter haiku work entitled, *Frozen Haiku* is a thought-provoking collection of imaginative, visually stunning haiku. This collection explores the magical transformations, discoveries, and interactions with nature as winter tightens her grip over the sleeping landscape.

haiku yellow

Introduction

Haiku Yellow is a breathtaking collection of stunning images captured and written in haiku verse from the contemporary English poet P.J. Reed. This collection explores the excitement and drama as the yellow of springtime bursts through the bleakness of winter throughout the Devon countryside.

The world in springtime is a joyful place full of possibilities and hope. P.J. Reed has looked into the beauty of a world reborn and clothed in yellow springtime glory. This study has resulted in a series of dramatic moments captured forever in her fresh, crisp verse.

In traditional Japanese haiku the poem has three lines, where the first and last lines contain five *moras*, while the middle line has seven. The *mora* is a unit of sound in the Japanese language, which is similar to a syllable, but not the same. The *moras* cannot be translated into English and therefore syllables are used in their place. When westernised, haiku is written as seventeen syllables divided into three lines of five, seven, and five syllables.

Traditional haiku does not rhyme or contain punctuation but have a juxtaposition on the first or third line dividing the poem into contrasting parts. The haiku is usually written with natural and seasonal references with feelings and thoughts succinctly captured in one breathe.

Westernised haiku has developed as a poetry form straying somewhat from the tight constraints of its traditional Japanese masters but still contains that moment of beauty encapsulated in three small lines.

Haiku Yellow

haiku yellow

Contents

haiku yellow

Haiku Yellow

Spring

Haiku Yellow

a blackbird listens
paused in her twig collection
woodpecker knocks twice

Haiku Yellow

a falling raindrop
splashes stone seeps into earth
what is failure

Haiku Yellow

a frowning sky smiled
people burst from houses tails
wagging in the sun

Haiku Yellow

a lone daffodil
waiting by a muddied lane
first touches of spring

and winter passes
the earth springs flower garlands
to welcome the sun

Haiku Yellow

bird songs after rain
a chorus of happiness
the wood is perfumed

Haiku Yellow

cool breezes whisper
softly to the sleeping earth
dandelion yawns

Haiku Yellow

drinking tea unpaired
old woman sits alone as
people hurry passed

Haiku Yellow

earth salutes the sun
the yellowness of springtime
painted on the green

Haiku Yellow

empty mountain winds
scatter thoughts of solitude
still the raven calls

Haiku Yellow

fresh storm stream hurries
bubbles gurgling over path
rain washed pebbles shine

Haiku Yellow

from darkness hidden
the shy moon appears and smiles
my soul companion

Haiku Yellow

frost bites are tamed as
lazing sun rises slowly
spreading yellow haze

Haiku Yellow

frowning thoughts circle
watch decisions best unmade
chase the empty clouds

gentle wind listens
to birdsongs of springtime love
winter is sleeping

Haiku Yellow

green fresh wrapped petals
burst through tired hedgerows bank
impetuous youth

Haiku Yellow

grass bound we wander
through dreams of thundering waves
the land gull and I

Haiku Yellow

gunnera ripples
giant leaves our umbrellas
caught by springs showers

helios watches
frost breaths melt in heating spring
summer sighs and stirs

Haiku Yellow

hiding in the blue
the watching moon surprised me
not alone today

Haiku Yellow

I climb my mountain
slopes crumble to dust and fall
purest summit calls

Haiku Yellow

I woke in winter
to find shy spring had tiptoed
green shoots in the white

Haiku Yellow

icy waters flow
sadness rolls across my soul
fog escapes the sea

in footsteps of one
noises of hanging silence
fill the emptiness

Haiku Yellow

left leaves cry and cling
to barren swaying branches
wind whispers be free

melancholia
silent sorrow hides in joy
as emotions fade

Haiku Yellow

moon hangs low tonight
she glows in silent beauty
the stars are hiding

Haiku Yellow

night time once more and
lonely moon asks for a friend
my bed lies empty

Haiku Yellow

pale moon is hiding
sadness falls as moonlight fails
path fades to darkness

Haiku Yellow

poor yellow flower
stands tall in her concrete crack
is this poverty

purple faces peer
shyly through the swaying grass
the gentle breeze smiles

raindrop melodies
seagull dancers pirouette
sing with hungry joy

Haiku Yellow

seconds tick slowly
as the moon falls from the sky
darkness hides away

Haiku Yellow

soft shoots are bursting
from the yawning hedgerows
hopefulness of youth

Haiku Yellow

soft winds blow gently
as rippling grasses murmur
summer is rising

Haiku Yellow

softly cooing songs
gentle pairs of preening doves
I am only one

sounds of solitude
as crumbling leaves shatter
while a lone bird sings

spring wind lies sleeping
birdsongs ring through the stillness
the hedge is tweeting

Haiku Yellow

stars flicker and fall
from the blue of midnight skies
past friends fade away

Haiku Yellow

sun falls from the sky
lost seconds hang in the air
waiting for your smile

sun rises slowly
wind whispers spring is coming
to the melting earth

swan couples dancing
symmetry in devotion
whispered love unheard

Haiku Yellow

the cold homeless man
cries buy a big issue please
dog lies on warm coat

Haiku Yellow

the dandelion
crowned white in ageless wisdom
grasses whisper praise

the death of winter
sparrows sing his eulogy
snowdrops bow their heads

the earth is springing
sheep sing a woolly chorus
bird songs are soaring

Haiku Yellow

the green is twisting
bending towards the yellow
a private journey

the night is falling
but darkness leaves no footsteps
silence in stillness

Haiku Yellow

the sadness of age
falling memories tumble
stolen by cold rains

Haiku Yellow

umbrellas flying
playful breeze blows and snatches
windblown shoppers squeal

Haiku Yellow

whispers of summer
ferns uncurl and leaves unwrap
bathing in the sun

Haiku Yellow

winters cruelest touch
heartbreak of a love unloved
thaws in warm embrace

Haiku Yellow

yellow ball rises
body reddens slowly wilts
heating shadows hide

Acknowledgements

'a lone daffodil' from *Haiku Nation*, (Lost Tower Publications, 2015) © P.J. Reed 2015. 'and winter passes' from *Frozen Haiku*, (Lost Tower Publications, 2016) © P.J. Reed 2016. 'cool breezes whisper' from *Haiku Nation*, (Lost Tower Publications, 2015) © P.J. Reed 2015. 'earth salutes the sun' from *Haiku Nation*, (Lost Tower Publications, 2015) © P.J. Reed 2015. 'fresh storm cloud hurries' from *Frozen Haiku*, (Lost Tower Publications, 2016) © P.J. Reed 2016. 'gunnera ripples' from *Haiku Nation*, (Lost Tower Publications, 2015) © P.J. Reed 2015. 'I woke in winter' from *Frozen Haiku*, (Lost Tower Publications, 2016) © P.J. Reed 2016. 'night time once more and' from *Haiku Nation*, (Lost Tower Publications, 2015) © P.J. Reed 2015. 'poor yellow flower' from *Haiku Nation*, (Lost Tower Publications, 2015) © P.J. Reed 2015. 'purple faces pear' from *Haiku Nation,* (Lost Tower Publications, 2015) © P.J. Reed 2015. 'seconds tick slowly' from *Frozen Haiku*, (Lost Tower Publications, 2016) © P.J. Reed 2016. 'softly cooing songs' from *Haiku Nation*, (Lost Tower Publications, 2015) © P.J. Reed 2015. 'stars flicker and fail' from *cattails*, (January Issue 2016) © P.J. Reed 2015. 'the dandelion' from *Haiku Nation*, (Lost Tower Publications, 2015) © P.J. Reed 2015.

Art

Haiku Yellow

44839502R00045

Printed in Poland
by Amazon Fulfillment
Poland Sp. z o.o., Wrocław